# The Pros and Cons of
# NUCLEAR POWER

## Ewan McLeish

rosen publishing's
rosen
central

New York

Published in 2008 by The Rosen Publishing Group, Inc.
29 East 21st Street, New York, NY 10010

First Edition

Series Editor: Jennifer Schofield
Editor: Debbie Foy
Consultant: Rob Bowden
Designer: Jane Hawkins
Cover designer: Paul Cherrill
Picture Researcher: Diana Morris
Illustrator: Ian Thompson
Indexer: Sue Lightfoot

Picture Acknowledgments:
Yann Arthus-Bertrand/Corbis: 10, 31. Bettmann/Corbis: 9.
Martin Bond/Still Pictures; 42. Rob Bowden/EASI-Images: 5, 28.
Bogdan Cristel/Reuters/Corbis: 32. Peter Dannatt/Ecoscene: 17.
Reinhard Dirscherl/Ecoscene: 38. Fred Dott/Still Pictures; 41.
Graham Neden/Ecoscene: 7. Tony Page/Ecoscene: 36.
Photri/Topfoto: 14. Picturepoint/Topham: 34. Roger Ressmeyer/
Corbis: front cover, 12, 23, 25. Sipa Press/Rex Features: 19.
Soeren Stache/dpa/Corbis: 27. Mike Whittle/Ecoscene: 6.
Tim Wright/Corbis: 1.

Library of Congress Cataloging-in-Publication Data

McLeish, Ewan, 1950-
  the pros and cons of Nuclear power / Ewan McLeish.
     p. cm. --  (The energy debate)
  Includes index.
  ISBN-13: 978-1-4042-3740-7 (library binding)
  ISBN-10: 1-4042-3740-2 (library binding)
  1.  Nuclear energy--Juvenile literature. 2.  Nuclear accidents--Juvenile literature.  I. Title.
  TK9148.M356 2007
  333.792'4--dc22

                                    2006039063

Manufactured in China

CPSIA Compliance Information: Batch #WAW0102YA: For Further Information contact Rosen Publishing, New York, New York at 1-800-237-9932

# Contents

## CHAPTER 1 | Nuclear power and the energy debate

Almost everything we do, from cooking a meal to catching a bus or turning on a light, uses a source of energy. Much of the energy we use comes in the form of electricity. However, traditional energy sources, such as oil and gas, are diminishing or becoming too expensive, and many countries are becoming concerned about their future energy supplies. The prospect of global warming hangs heavily over all parts of the world, rich or poor, and it is clear that we need to seriously consider alternative sources of energy on a worldwide scale. This book looks at the pros and cons of obtaining that energy from the atom—from nuclear power.

### A memorable accident
On April 26, 1986, a safety test at the nuclear power station in Chernobyl, U.S.S.R. (now Ukraine) went disastrously wrong. Instead of shutting down, as it was supposed to do, there was a massive surge of power, causing the reactor to overheat and explode. A huge cloud of radioactive dust drifted northwest across much of Eastern and then Northern Europe, contaminating more than 770,00 sq miles (200,000 square kilometers) of land. Millions watched and waited as the world's worst nuclear accident unfolded.

❝ We were engineers, and we were trained in what the reactors could or could not do, and what could go wrong. We were prepared for fire and other things, but we were not prepared for this. ❞

Alexander Yuvchenko, senior engineer-mechanic, Chernobyl nuclear power plant

### A climate in crisis
On September 20, 2002, the hanging Kolka Glacier in Southern Russia collapsed. Over 3,500 million cubic feet (100 million cubic meters) of ice and debris thundered down the slopes of Mount Dzhimarai-Khokh, leaving a 15-mile (24-kilometer) trail of destruction. Small villages were obliterated and 125 people died. The world was waking up to a new danger. The ice caps were melting. Global warming was becoming a reality.

### The debate
In many ways, these two stories illustrate what the energy debate is about. How can we obtain the energy we need without damaging the planet and ourselves in the process?

As we shall see, the generation of energy to supply our homes, our vehicles, and our industries, comes at a cost. If we continue to burn traditional fossil fuels (coal, oil, and gas) in our power stations, vehicles, and factories, global temperatures are likely to keep rising as a result of global warming. If we move more toward other sources of energy, such as nuclear power, we could possibly halt the effects of global warming on a significant scale. However, nuclear power comes with its own set of problems. Many people would argue we should be moving away from both!

▽  We are accustomed to using large amounts of electricity. This power has to be generated, and all methods of generation, including nuclear power, are potentially damaging.

This book looks at what is called "the nuclear option." Should the world continue to expand nuclear technology and develop new generations of nuclear power stations? Or does our experience so far tell us we should be looking elsewhere for future energy needs? In order to make this decision, we need to understand what nuclear power is really about.

◁ Nuclear power plant at Sellafield, England. The spherical construction is the containment building that houses the nuclear reactor. The cooling towers are on the extreme left.

## Cheap energy—at a price?

The nuclear energy industry has undergone many changes in the half century or so during which it has been operating. When the first nuclear power stations went into commercial production in the mid 1950s, it was confidently stated that the electricity it produced would be "too cheap to meter." The general public had very little understanding of the technology involved, and for awhile, it did appear that nuclear power would meet many of the world's present and future energy needs.

However, doubts soon began to arise about the true costs of nuclear power when the safety aspects of nuclear power stations also became an issue. Seven years before the accident at Chernobyl, a cooling malfunction in a reactor at the Three Mile Island power station in Pennsylvania, caused a partial "meltdown" of the reactor core. Although no significant amounts of radioactivity were released, it became clear that a major disaster was only narrowly avoided. In addition to this, the question of how to get rid of the radioactive waste, produced as a by-

## Global power

There are 441 commercial nuclear power stations in the world today, operating in 31 different countries. They generate over 16 percent of the world's electricity, and 24 percent of electricity in what are known as the OECD (Organisation for Economic Cooperation and Development) countries—the richer parts of the world, such as the United States, Europe, and Japan. Today, a total of 17 countries depend on nuclear power for at least a quarter of their electricity. France and Lithuania get around three-quarters of their power from nuclear energy. Belgium, Bulgaria, Slovakia, South Korea, Sweden, Switzerland, Slovenia, and Ukraine all get a third or more. The U.S. gets one- fifth of its energy from nuclear power.

product of nuclear power, was causing increasing concern. The nuclear power industry appeared to be in trouble.

## The issue of global warming

For years, scientists had been warning that emissions of carbon dioxide ($CO_2$) from burning fossil fuels were beginning to raise global temperatures. The conventional power stations, running on fossil fuels, make a significant contribution to overall carbon emissions. Nuclear power produces less carbon than fossil fuels. Could it be the answer? Suddenly, the nuclear industry appeared to be back in business.

▽ A glacier meets the sea and crashes into the water. The rate at which the polar icecaps are melting is increasing. Most scientists now believe this is a result of global warming.

### CASE STUDY: Retreating glaciers

The first full survey of all 244 glaciers in the Antarctic Peninsula was completed in 2005. The investigation showed that 87 percent of the glaciers have retreated over the past 50 years, and they are retreating by an average of 165 feet (50 meters) a year. One, the Widdowson glacier, is losing more than a half a mile per year. Nothing similar is believed to have happened for at least 2,000 years. Researchers link the retreat to exceptional warming of the air around the peninsula, five times the average for Antarctica.

# CHAPTER 2 How is energy generated from the atom?

A pellet of nuclear fuel weighs roughly 0.1 ounces (6 grams). This is about half the weight of a typical front door key. And yet it can yield the same amount of energy as a ton (tonne) of coal. How can this be possible?

## The atom explained

Atoms are the tiny particles from which all matter is made. Too small even to be seen under an electron microscope, it would take around a billion atoms to cover the period at the end of this sentence. However, atoms are not the smallest particles.

Atoms are made up of a dense nucleus surrounded by a "sea" of negatively charged particles called *electrons*. The nucleus itself is made up of two further types of particle—protons and neutrons. Protons are all positively charged, so in theory, they should be flying apart in the same way that similar poles of magnets repel each other. The fact that the particles do not fly apart is due to something called the *strong nuclear force*. This acts as a kind of atomic "glue" that holds protons and neutrons together.

## Splitting the atom

Although the technology is immensely complicated, it is possible to overcome this strong nuclear force. One way of doing this is to bombard atoms with a constant stream of neutrons. Under

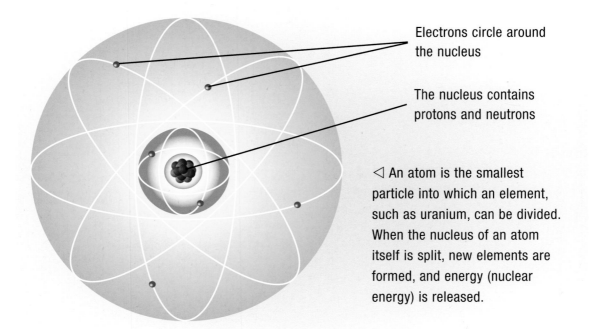

Electrons circle around the nucleus

The nucleus contains protons and neutrons

◁ An atom is the smallest particle into which an element, such as uranium, can be divided. When the nucleus of an atom itself is split, new elements are formed, and energy (nuclear energy) is released.

the right conditions, this process splits the atom in two—liberating energy in the process as heat. This is what is meant by *nuclear fission*.

The amount of heat liberated by splitting a single atom is minute. But if we multiply this millions or billions of times, then we start to liberate some serious energy—nuclear energy.

## Unstable atoms

Only certain kinds of atoms are suitable for nuclear fission. These tend to be large, unstable atoms (such as uranium) that decay naturally into other types of atoms (such as thorium and radium), giving off radiation in the process. These types of atoms are called *radioactive isotopes*, or simply *radioisotopes*.

Isotopes are simply heavier or lighter versions of the same type of atom. Uranium, the main nuclear fuel, is the heaviest element found in trace, or tiny, amounts in nature. It is found in a type of mineral ore known as *pitchblende*, which is about 1 percent uranium oxide. Uranium occurs in two main forms (or isotopes): uranium 235 (U-235) and uranium 238 (U-238). Only U-235 is suitable for splitting, but this makes up less than a hundredth of the total uranium present. This means that, in most kinds of nuclear reactor, the U-235 has to be concentrated, or enriched, before it can be formed into pellets and used as nuclear fuel.

## CASE STUDY: Einstein and nuclear weapons

The German scientist, Albert Einstein developed the equation E = mc2 to show that mass could be converted into energy. In 1939, Einstein wrote to President Roosevelt, warning him that Nazi Germany might develop devastating weapons based on his equation. As a result, Roosevelt put money into building an atomic bomb, which was finally used against Japan. Einstein was so horrified that he later devoted much of his life to campaigning against nuclear weapons.

## Chain reaction

Nuclear fission requires an atom of U-235 to be struck by a neutron, releasing a tiny amount of heat energy. However, what is needed are millions or billions of such collisions. When a neutron hits a uranium atom, the uranium nucleus becomes unstable and splits into two smaller nuclei, releasing two or three more neutrons in the process. These neutrons go on to collide with other uranium atoms, causing them to split, liberating more neutrons, and so on, until millions of neutrons are colliding with millions of uranium atoms. Now huge amounts of energy are being released—there is a chain reaction underway. This is what is happening in the heart (or core) of a nuclear reactor.

## From heat to electricity

This heat energy needs to be harnessed to produce electricity. Depending on the type of nuclear reactor involved, the heat generated in the reactor is transferred to a coolant—either water or a gas, such as $CO_2$. The coolant is

▽ Inside the core of a nuclear reactor, the fuel rods are bombarded with neutrons, causing the atoms to split in a controlled chain reaction.

usually pumped through a heat exchanger, where it transfers its energy to more water, creating high-pressure steam. The steam is used to turn turbines, which are then used to power a generator—producing electricity in exactly the same way as a traditional coal-fired power station.

## Control rods

What stops the chain reaction from running out of control as more and more neutrons are liberated? In the core of the reactor, the uranium oxide pellets are packed into long columns called *fuel rods*. Placed between the fuel rods is another type of rod made of boron or cadmium that absorb neutrons. Raising or lowering these rods into the core of the reactor controls the rate of nuclear fission by soaking up neutrons. Unsurprisingly, these are known as the *control rods*.

Finally, surrounding the fuel rods and control rods is the moderator, which is usually water or graphite. This slows down the fast-moving neutrons, so they are more likely to collide with uranium atoms, rather than escape.

## Containment of radiation

Nuclear fission is a potentially dangerous process. It is accompanied by the release of harmful gamma and alpha radiation, while the fission products (formed when the uranium

**❝❝** It is most curious; when I irradiate uranium with neutrons, I only succeed in obtaining isotopes of barium, when you would expect much heavier elements. **❞❞**

Letter from the scientist Otto Hahn to his colleague Lise Meitner. Hahn expected the neutrons to be added to the uranium atoms. Meitner realized that the uranium atoms were being split into lighter elements.

atoms are split) are also highly radioactive. Fission products include radioisotopes of barium, krypton, caesium, and strontium. Alpha and gamma radiation are both known as *ionizing radiation*. This means that they can change neutral atoms into charged particles. In body cells, this can mean the formation of cancers and the development of mutations.

The nuclear reactor is usually housed in a pressure vessel, which is a strong steel structure containing the reactor core, the moderator, and the coolant. This is placed inside a containment building, designed to prevent damage from the outside and to stop radiation from escaping, either as part of normal operations or in an accident.

## Atomic testing

On July 16, 1945, the world's first atomic test was successfully carried out at the Alamogordo Test Range in the desert in New Mexico. Observing the test from the comparative safety of a concrete bunker several miles away, its designer, the scientist Robert Oppenheimer, watched it in awe.

Three weeks later, as World War II (1939–1945) continued to rage in the Far East, the first atomic bomb was dropped on the Japanese city of Hiroshima, instantly killing 140,000 people. Three days after this, a similar device was dropped on the city of Nagasaki. The war was over.

△ An atomic explosion takes place on a Pacific atoll. The control of this destructive energy led to the development of nuclear power.

" We knew the world would never be the same. A few people laughed, a few people cried, most were silent. I remembered the line from the Hindu scripture, the Bhagavad-Gita, "Now, I am become Death, the destroyer of the worlds." I suppose we all thought that, one way or another. "

Robert Oppenheimer, atomic physicist

The atomic bombs dropped on Hiroshima and Nagasaki were created by runaway chain reactions (or uncontrolled nuclear fission). In this case, plutonium rather than uranium was used. Atomic scientists realized that if all that destructive force, released in a few seconds, could be controlled, a new source of energy would be available and could be harnessed for peaceful purposes. And so it was that nuclear power was born.

## Nuclear power expands

The very first nuclear power station to supply electricity to a national grid began operation at Calder Hall, England, in 1956. The first commercial plant in the United States opened four years later. Other nuclear facilities followed rapidly around the world. Today, in addition to the 31 countries producing commercial nuclear power, 20 other countries operate "civil" research reactors, which are used for scientific purposes. Nuclear reactors also power hundreds of naval vessels, including nuclear submarines.

## Which way to go?

We are now at a crucial point in our search to find safe and secure energy supplies to carry us through the present century and beyond. Nuclear power stations, like any other electricity generators, can be operated only for a certain period of time,

and this is usually around 50 years. After this, they become outdated and unsafe. Many of our existing nuclear power stations will come to the end of their working lives within the next 15 to 20 years. To design and build new ones will take almost as long. We are standing at a crossroads.

### THE ARGUMENT: We should invest in a nuclear future

**For:**
- Nuclear technology has already been developed and is available.
- Oil and gas supplies are running out. If we delay making a decision about building new nuclear power stations, many countries will find themselves facing an "energy gap" in 20 years' time.

**Against:**
- Better and safer technologies are already available, and these technologies must now be considered.
- How nuclear waste is dealt with now will have vital consequences for the world as a whole for hundreds, or even thousands, of years to come.

# CHAPTER 3 | Putting nuclear power to work

Like any technology, the design of nuclear power stations is constantly changing. Factors, such as cost, safety, and availability of fuel, all influence what type of design is chosen.

## Water pressure

By far, the most common nuclear power station design is the Pressurized Water Reactor (or PWR), favored by the United States, France, Japan, and Russia. It is also the design used to power nuclear submarines and other naval vessels. PWRs use enriched uranium oxide as fuel, in which U-235 is concentrated from 0.7 percent to about 3.5 to 5.0 percent. Water acts as the coolant. Boiling Water Reactors (BWRs) are similar, but the coolant powers the turbines directly rather than passing through a heat exchanger.

▽ The control rods of a gas-cooled nuclear reactor that is under construction.

During this process, the turbines also become radioactive, and therefore they also have to have some shielding to prevent the escape of radiation.

## Gas-cooled

Another commonly used design is the Gas-cooled Reactor, used mainly by the U.K. As the name suggests, these reactors use $CO_2$, rather than water, as a coolant. There are two main types. Early models were called *Magnox* reactors, before the design was modified to produce Advanced Gas-cooled Reactors (or AGRs). Magnox reactors were powered by the natural, rather than the enriched, form of uranium (U-235 present at only 0.7 percent). In AGRs, the uranium is enriched to about 3 percent.

## "Heavy" water

Other designs also exist. Canada, for example, uses a nuclear reactor in which the moderator (the material used to slow down the neutrons, to increase the likelihood of collisions with uranium atoms) is "heavy" water. Heavy water is water in which the hydrogen atoms have neutrons added to the nucleus. This makes the water atoms "heavier," and therefore more effective in slowing down the passage of neutrons. Like Magnox reactors, these so-called "CANDU" or Pressurized Heavy Water Reactors, use natural uranium oxide as fuel.

## Fast-moving neutrons

Russia, on the other hand, has developed a number of Light Water Graphite Reactors, in which the moderator is graphite and the fuel is enriched uranium. Finally, Japan, France, and Russia also have a small number of Fast Neutron or Fast Breeder Reactors (or FBRs), which use both plutonium and uranium oxide as fuel. There is no moderator, so they work using fast-moving neutrons. They are capable of generating massive amounts of energy, but are also very expensive to run.

## CASE STUDY: Natural reactor

The world's only known natural reactor "switched itself on" nearly two billion years ago, and then turned on and off like a geyser for about 150,000 years. The concentration of U-235 in rocks at Oklo in Gabon, West Africa, was so high that it triggered sustained nuclear fission, generating an average power of about 100 kilowatts. The concentration of isotopes in the rocks suggests the reactor switched on for about 30 minutes, then lay dormant for 2½ hours before switching on again.

## Uranium all around us

Uranium is a naturally radioactive metal that occurs throughout the Earth's crust. It is not particularly rare, perhaps 500 times as abundant as gold and about as common as tin. It is present in tiny amounts in most rocks and soils, as well as in rivers and seawater. Natural uranium itself is not highly radioactive, but is decaying constantly into other elements, many of which are also radioactive, such as radium and radon gas.

In some areas of the world, the concentration of uranium in rocks is high enough to make its extraction for fuel worthwhile. These areas include Canada, Niger, Namibia, Australia, and countries of the old Soviet Union such as Russia, Kazakhstan, and Ukraine. In the same way as coal, most uranium extraction is by underground or open pit mining.

## Mining for uranium

Open pit mines require the removal of huge amounts of earth and rock, usually by large earth-moving vehicles. Underground mines require the building of access tunnels and shafts, but cause fewer disturbances and remove less material than open pit mines. Conditions for uranium miners, however, can be extremely hazardous.

## CASE STUDY: Mining in Namibia

In November 2005, Namibia opened its second uranium mine, despite strong opposition from environmental groups. The Langer Heinrich mine is situated within the protected Namib Naukluft Park in the Namib desert. An Australian company owns the mine and has been awarded a 25-year mining license by Namibia's Ministry of Mining and Energy. Opposition groups are concerned about water pollution, radioactive dust, and the emission of radon, a highly radioactive gas. They also fear that people visiting the park, which is a major tourist attraction, would be exposed to risk. In addition, the mine would become the country's single largest consumer of water, which is a scarce resource in Namibia. However, supporters of the mine point out that it will employ about 100 workers and generate around $48 million per year in export income.

A recent study found that the former East Germany's 400,000 uranium miners suffered at least a 10 percent increased risk of developing lung cancer due to radiation exposure.

## A better way?

In recent years, there has been increased use of a method of extraction called *solution mining*. Oxygenated water is pumped through the ore where the rock is particularly porous. The water is made slightly acid or alkaline, depending on the type of rock present, so that the uranium ore dissolves and can then be extracted from the solution. This results in little surface disturbance, and no waste rock (or tailings) is produced. Once the uranium has been removed, the solution is pumped back into the rock and used again. The excess solution has to be treated as radioactive waste and is injected into special disposal wells. Around 16 percent of world uranium production is by solution mining, and this occurs mostly in the United States and Australia.

▽ An open pit uranium mine in Australia. The terraced walls prevent collapse, but increase the area covered by the mine.

## "Yellowcake"

Getting the uranium out of the ground is only the beginning of a long journey to the nuclear reactor. If the uranium has been mined, it has to be extracted from the ore (or rock) in which it is contained. This is known as milling.

In a mill, the ore is ground up and the uranium is extracted by dissolving it in strong acid or alkali. The uranium is removed from the solution and dried out to form what is known as "yellowcake." This concentrate normally contains about 80 percent uranium (the original ore may contain as little as 0.1 percent uranium). It is then packed into 50-gallon (200-liter) drums ready for transportation. Worldwide production of yellowcake is currently around 69,300 tons (70,500 tonnes) per year, but this is likely to rise as Central Asian nations like Kazakhstan begin to expand their uranium-mining industries.

Meanwhile, the rock tailings, which still contain most of the radioactivity of the original deposit as well as toxic heavy metals, have to be buried in pits nearby. The pits used are usually worked-out mines. The United States' government, however, had to shift 10.8 million tons (11 million tonnes) of uranium tailings from the banks of the Colorado river to a site 30 miles (48 kilometers) away in order to prevent the leaching of toxic chemicals into the water supply.

## THE ARGUMENT: Uranium mining is dangerous

### For:
- Uranium mining and extraction is no worse than other mining operations.
- The rock waste is less radioactive than the original rock from which the uranium has been removed.

### Against:
- Uranium waste dumps have been shown to contaminate local food and water supplies.
- In Kyrgyzstan, radium left behind by two decades of uranium mining has exposed local people to 40 times the internationally recommended safety limit.
- Mining areas are subject to landslides and earthquakes.

## Enriching the product

As we saw on pages 14–15, most designs of nuclear reactor require an enriched form of uranium. This is because fissile or "splittable" uranium (U-235) makes up only 0.7 percent of the total uranium present in a

△ A uranium enrichment plant, involving the use of high-speed centrifuges that separate U-235 from U-238. It is a complex process, because the centrifuges must be synchronized in a "cascade effect" for enrichment to be successful.

natural sample. The remainder is mainly the more stable U-238.

During the enrichment process, the uranium is refined to a stage where it can be used in nuclear reactors that run on natural uranium.

The remaining uranium is converted into a form that allows the majority of the U-238 to be progressively removed, so increasing the concentration of U-235 to between 3.5 and 5 percent.

Finally, the enriched uranium is compressed at very high temperatures to produce ceramic pellets, or fuel pellets. These fuel pellets are encased inside thin metal tubes (usually made of zirconium, which allows neutrons to pass through easily) and assembled into bundles to form fuel rods.

## Completing the cycle

The uranium in the fuel rods needs a "critical mass" to sustain itself and keep fission going. The chain reaction dies down long before all of the U-235 has been used up. At the same time, although the U-238 in the fuel pellet does not undergo fission, it can absorb neutrons. This converts the U-238 into a substance that is a lot more difficult to deal with—plutonium (Pu). The "spent" fuel rods now contain around 1 percent U-235 (compared to the original 3.5 to 5 percent), 1 percent plutonium, and the radioactive products of the fission reaction itself, such as radioisotopes of caesium, strontium, and krypton (about 3 percent). The rest is mainly U-238. All of these must be dealt with, and one method is to reprocess the spent fuel into a form that can be reused.

▽ After extraction, the uranium oxide is converted into a gas (uranium hexafluoride—$UF_6$) before being enriched. Spent fuel may be stored in glass (vitrification) before storage and final disposal. Reprocessed uranium (U) goes back into the conversion process, while plutonium (Pu) can be used directly in fuel fabrication.

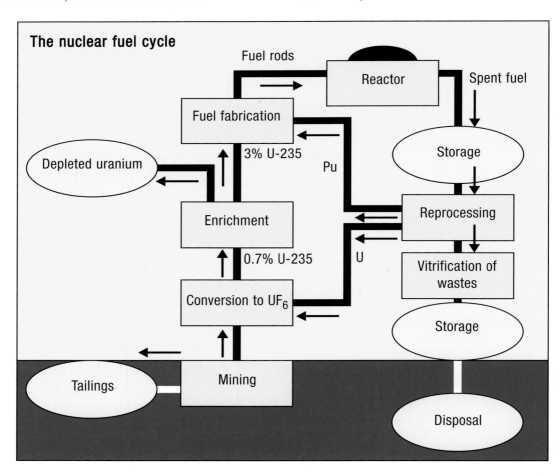

**The nuclear fuel cycle**

Fuel rods

Reactor

Spent fuel

Fuel fabrication

3% U-235

Pu

Storage

Depleted uranium

Enrichment

0.7% U-235

U

Reprocessing

Vitrification of wastes

Conversion to $UF_6$

Storage

Tailings

Mining

Disposal

## Dealing with used fuel

But how can fuel be used twice? The answer is not quite as strange as it might sound. First, the spent fuel is removed from the reactor, usually after between 12 and 24 months. This requires the reactor to be shut down for a period of time, while about a third of the fuel rods are replaced.

When removed from the reactor, the fuel rods will be emitting both nuclear radiation and heat. The used fuel is unloaded into storage or cooling ponds, which are usually located next to the reactor, to allow radiation levels to decrease and to remove some of the heat. Used fuel can be held in these ponds for several months to years, again depending on its radioactivity. The used fuel can either be reprocessed or prepared for permanent disposal.

## Reprocessing fuel

In a reprocessing facility, the used fuel is separated into "fractions," and the U-235 and plutonium is processed into fresh fuel. This reduces the amount of waste produced, although much of it is highly radioactive. The reprocessed uranium can then be enriched again, while the plutonium can be used directly in Fast Breeder Reactors, or can be mixed with the uranium to make mixed oxide fuel (or MOX) in a fuel fabrication plant. This can be used in most types of reactor.

**THE ARGUMENT: Reprocessing reduces the need for uranium mining**

**For:**
- Recycling or reprocessing uranium from spent fuel means that less uranium has to be dug out of the ground.
- Recycling also reduces the problem of what to do with the waste products in the spent fuel.

**Against:**
- Reprocessing creates highly radioactive by-products, which still have to be dealt with.
- It is technically possible, although difficult to do, to use reprocessed plutonium to build nuclear weapons.

Although reprocessing does extend the life of nuclear fuel, like the fossil fuels—coal, gas, and oil—uranium is a finite, or nonrenewable, resource. Depending on how quickly it is used, and how much of it is reprocessed or regenerated as plutonium, uranium reserves will run out eventually.

## Safe waste disposal

We have seen that throughout the nuclear fuel cycle, radioactive waste is an inevitable by-product. This may be the rock tailings produced during mining operations, the waste water produced in solution mining, the extraction of the uranium from its ore, or the by-products of the nuclear reactor operation itself, including the job of reprocessing. Whatever it is, it has to be disposed of safely.

> ❝ People won't accept nuclear power until you deal with the waste. It is a problem that lasts for so long; it becomes a moral issue. ❞
>
> Professor Martin Dove, Cambridge-MIT Institute, England

Not all radioactive waste is the same, however. The difference between high-, intermediate-, and low-level wastes, as well as half-life needs to be clear.

## Radioactive decay

All radioactive materials have a particular half-life—the time it takes for half the radioactive atoms present in the material to decay into some other element (which may also be radioactive). Expressed in simple terms, *half-life* is the time it takes for a piece of radioactive material to become half as radioactive. If an element has a half-life of an hour, it will be half as radioactive after that hour, a quarter as radioactive after the next hour, and so on.

The half-lives of different radioactive elements vary enormously, literally from seconds to billions of years. U-238 has a half-life of 4.5 billion years, whereas U-235 has a more modest half-life of 704 million years. Different isotopes of plutonium have shorter half-lives, between 88 and 37,600 years. It is obvious, then, that material with a long half-life will remain radioactive for longer than material with a short half-life.

## A question of level

Different types of radioactive material also produce different types and intensities (or levels) of radiation. In turn, these require different waste management techniques. High-level radioactive waste produces the most intense (and therefore dangerous) radiation, including both alpha and gamma radiation. High-level waste includes the products of nuclear fission and reprocessing. Intermediate-level waste is also produced during nuclear reactor operation and reprocessing.

Low-level radioactive waste—the least harmful type—is produced at all stages of the nuclear fuel cycle, including mining and extraction.

## Level versus half-life

The half-life and the level of radiation of a substance are clearly not the same thing. In fact, they tend to work in opposition to each other. Most high-level wastes will tend to have a relatively short half-life. This is because they are decaying very rapidly, giving off high levels of radiation. For example, the level of radioactivity and heat from used fuel falls by about 1,000 times within 40 years, giving an average half-life of about four years. On the other hand, low-level materials, such as U-238 and U-235, have half-lives of millions or billions of years, because they are decaying slowly and giving off very little radiation. Understanding this difference is important when looking at the problems of disposal.

▷ These drums contain low-level radioactive waste ready for burial, which could be clothing, laboratory equipment, and building materials.

| CHAPTER 4 |
| --- |

# Nuclear power and the environment

The question of the safety of nuclear power has troubled the industry, almost since it began. Is this fear justified? After all, we are exposed to "background radiation" all the time—from space, the rocks around us, hospital X-rays, building materials, even our food. Although the worst nuclear accident in peacetime, the Chernobyl explosion, appears to have caused fewer deaths than predicted. But many people are still feeling its effects.

## The problem of waste

The disposal of nuclear waste is one of the most difficult issues for the industry. Although some low- and intermediate-level waste is currently disposed of underground, there are still no permanent disposal facilities in which high-level waste, such as used nuclear fuel, and the waste from reprocessing can be placed. The 282,000 tons (287,000 tonnes) of spent fuel and fission products that now exist worldwide are currently still in cooling ponds ready to be stored in glass (called *vitrification*) before final disposal. All of it is above ground.

Many of these temporary storage facilities are running out of space. In the U.S., some cooling ponds are so densely packed that the fuel rods have to be separated by neutron-absorbing boron panels to prevent the spent fuel from restarting a chain reaction. The International Atomic Energy Agency (IAEA) estimates that, by 2020, there will be 482,000 tons (490,000 tonnes) of spent fuel. Existing facilities and new sites will not be able to hold it all. Above ground, the waste could also be the target of terrorist attacks. Underground storage seems to be the only solution. But is this any safer? Once underground, it is difficult to monitor changes in the state of the nuclear material and difficult to reach it, if problems occur.

> " Final (effectively underground) disposal of high level wastes is required in due course, but there is no technological or logistical reason why this is urgent. Rather the contrary, the longer the HL waste is in storage, the easier it is to handle safely. "
>
> World Nuclear Association 2005

## A matter of opinion?

Many supporters of nuclear power
do not see burial as a pressing need.
We have already seen that most high-
level waste has a fairly short half-life.
In theory, at least, it could return to
fairly normal levels in 50 or 100 years
(although some people would consider
that a long time!). This is not true of
all such waste, however. One estimate
suggests that it will take 100,000 years
before all the current nuclear waste
will return to the same level of
radioactivity as natural uranium.

△ Overseeing high-level radioactive waste.
Full protective suits and respirators protect the
workers from breathing in harmful particles.

Other estimates suggest 10,000 years.
While it is true that the volume of
high-level waste is low compared
with other levels of waste (less than
1 percent by volume), it contains over
95 percent of the total radioactivity!
Opinions on how to dispose of it may
differ; most agree, however, that the
safety of many future generations
needs to be taken into account.

## Burying waste

Where can high-level radioactive waste be buried? Ideally, a stable, dry site is needed, since a leaking container could allow radioactivity to find its way into ground water. Unfortunately, there are very few areas of the world where radioactive waste can be buried in dry places—especially those guaranteed to stay dry for the next 10,000 to 100,000 years. Nuclear scientists in Germany are currently investigating the idea of burying nuclear waste in what are known as *salt domes*. These are almost impermeable to water. The U.S. Department of Energy is developing a dry storage facility in the Yucca Mountains in Nevada. Here, it is planned that 83,600 tons (85,000 tonnes) of high-level radioactive waste could be buried 1,000 feet (300 meters) below the surface. Very little water is expected to seep through cracks in the rocks—any that does should be evaporated by heat from the waste itself.

## THE ARGUMENT: Storing radioactive waste is not a problem

### For:

• Radioactive waste has been stored without any real problems in many countries since the 1950s.

• It could go on being stored above ground indefinitely, if necessary.

### Against:

• There are simply not enough facilities to go on storing high-level waste above ground, and new waste is being added all the time.

• If it is stored underground, the safety of the site cannot be guaranteed for thousands of years.

## Test case

The problems surrounding the deep burial of radioactive waste are enormous. At the Aspö Hard Rock Laboratory in Sweden, atomic researchers have buried six full-sized "test" canisters 20 feet (6 meters) long and 26.5 tons (27 tonnes each), 1,475 feet (450 meters) down into the earth. The canisters are coated with rust-resistant copper and lowered into vertical shafts lined with clay to protect them from running water and earthquakes. The burial site is fitted with sensors to measure the temperature, water movement, tension in the rock walls, and bacterial action. The canisters are also fitted with electric heaters to create the heating effect of real radioactive decay. The scientists' goal is to predict what could happen in the event of real radioactive waste burial.

△ Engineers inspect the wall of a nuclear waste facility, where fuel rods are stored until they can be recycled or disposed of permanently.

## CASE STUDY:
## Aspö Hard Rock Laboratory

A quarter of a mile (1.6 kilometers) below ground, a lift shaft leads to a massive metal door, over three feet (0.9 meters) thick. Beyond the door is a huge hall that has been blasted out of the granite. Leading from it are a labyrinth of roads and tunnels. This is Sweden's Aspö Hard Rock Laboratory. In 2017, this will probably become the world's first permanent underground nuclear disposal site. Perhaps surprisingly, there is the constant drip of running water. This might seem like a bad idea for a permanent nuclear storage facility, but this water has taken 7,000 years to seep down from the earth's surface, and that means it is unlikely that radioactive material will leak out into any nearby watercourses and pollute them.

△ A crowded street in Seoul, the capital city of South Korea. Seoul is only 30 miles (50 km) from the North Korean border. It is alleged that South Korea may be developing its own nuclear weapon as a response to North Korean claims that it has built an atomic device.

## Nuclear weapons

We have already seen that nuclear power arose out of the race to build nuclear weapons. We also know that enriched uranium contains around 3 to 5 percent uranium. If this is boosted to over 90 percent, the material becomes suitable for making an atomic bomb. At least eight countries, including the U.S., Russia, France, Israel, Pakistan, and China, already possess the technology. Some of these countries are in politically unstable areas. North Korea, another highly unstable country, also claims to have nuclear weapons, and Iran may follow.

## The case of Iran

On April 11, 2006, the government of Iran announced an "historic" breakthrough. Iranian scientists had, for the first time, completed the nuclear fuel cycle by enriching uranium for use in nuclear power plants. Of course, enriching uranium is nothing new. But Iran has plenty of oil, so why would it need nuclear power? It is also located in a politically unstable part of the world. World leaders, including the United Nations, were concerned. They saw this as another step toward Iran securing nuclear weapons.

## "Dirty bomb"

In fact, there is already enough so-called "weapons grade" nuclear material available in the world to build more than 300,000 nuclear weapons. Much of this nuclear material is derived from the dismantling of existing nuclear weapons, but stores of plutonium are growing all the time. Not all of this material is well protected, and one concern is that terrorist groups may take advantage of its vulnerability.

> " Our first concern is the risk of nuclear terrorism. We worry about what could happen in Russia, Pakistan, India, and China... even the best-protected bank can be robbed. Someone, maybe an insider, could make off with something—and then we'll have hell to pay. "
>
> David Albright, Institute for Science and International Security, Washington D.C. September 7, 2005

In a "worst case" scenario, terrorists could seize enough nuclear material to trigger a nuclear explosion in a big city, killing perhaps several hundred thousand people instantly, and exposing millions more to radioactive contamination. Another, much more plausible scenario, is that stolen nuclear material could be used by terrorists to make a so-called "dirty bomb," using ordinary explosives. This would not cause a nuclear explosion, but it could spread highly radioactive material over a wide area.

## Attack from the air

Finally, suppose a group of determined terrorists were to fly a plane into a nuclear power station? Most existing reactor containment buildings are not strong enough to withstand the full impact of a large aircraft. The new European Pressurized Reactor being constructed in Olkiluoto in Finland, (see page 45) is designed to resist an accidental crash by a 4.9 ton (five-tonne) military fighter, and from this it is argued that the reactor could survive the impact of a much larger airliner (since the part of any aircraft inflicting most damage would be its engines). Even if this were true, an attack on cooling ponds could also be devastating. With the water draining off, the fuel cladding, made of zirconium alloy, would overheat and burst into flames, again causing serious and widespread contamination.

## Accident!

It is important to understand that the scenarios described on page 29 are unlikely, though not impossible. More likely is the occurrence of an accident at a nuclear power plant. We know this because accidents have already occurred. Some have been serious, such as the explosion at Chernobyl in 1986, others less so.

In August 2004, a high-pressure steam leak from a power turbine at the Mihama nuclear power plant in Japan killed four people. This time there was no leak of radiation, but in 1999, two workers died in an uncontrolled chain reaction at the Tokaimura nuclear power plant, north of Tokyo. This accident also led to the discovery that safety records at a number of nuclear power plants had been falsified.

> **"** We should not fan people's fears about the safety of nuclear power plants by overreacting to this accident. **"**
>
> *Yomiuri Shimbun* (Japan's largest daily newspaper, following the Mihama accident)

In May 2005, the U.K.'s Thermal Oxide Reprocessing Plant (THORPE) was closed following a leak of highly radioactive liquid containing 19.6 tons (20 tonnes) of plutonium and uranium dissolved in nitric acid. The reprocessing plant may never reopen. In other countries, where there is greater secrecy and records are hard to obtain, accidents (or near-accidents) may go unreported.

## Chernobyl—exaggerated claims?

What of the worst nuclear accident in history? It may be surprising that, as far as we know, less than 60 people have died as a result of the accident at Chernobyl. These were emergency workers, exposed to huge doses of radiation, who were trying to contain the damage immediately after the explosion. There have also been no recorded birth defects as a result of people in the area being exposed to radiation (radiation is known to cause cell damage, including that to eggs and sperm). Estimates of thousands of cancer deaths in the 20 to 30 years following the accident have not, so far, proved accurate. However, four thousand children who were exposed to the fallout have contracted thyroid cancer, although the vast majority are expected to survive. Currently figures of around 3,000 extra cancer deaths are still being predicted, but this total is constantly being downgraded. It now appears that the models used to predict cancer deaths were based on higher levels of radiation than were experienced by most people exposed to Chernobyl's radioactive cloud.

> Because of the difficulty of attributing specific cancers to radiation over decades, the precise number of deaths is unlikely ever to be known. "
>
> U.N./Chernobyl Forum report, 2005

## Newer is better?

It is also the case that the new generation of nuclear power stations will not only be more efficient than present ones, but will also be safer. On the other hand, as more and more countries embrace nuclear technology, many of which are poor and perhaps less able to deal with the problems and issues that nuclear power brings, it would be foolish to rule out the possibility of another accident—one that could make Chernobyl look insignificant by comparison.

▽ Reactor 3 at Chernobyl, Ukraine, after the explosion that wrecked reactor 4 in 1986 and spread radioactive dust over Eastern and Northern Europe. The last of Chernobyl's reactors closed in 2000.

## Public image

One issue on which both supporters and opponents of nuclear power would probably agree, is that nuclear power has an image problem. The idea of radiation, in particular, makes people understandably nervous. It cannot be seen or felt, but its effects can be terrible, as shown by the many victims of Hiroshima and Nagasaki who survived the initial blast, but died later of radiation sickness. Levels such as this would probably be experienced

△ Protesters from the environmental group Greenpeace demonstrate against a nuclear power facility on the River Danube, Romania.

only by large numbers of people in a nuclear war, however. It may be that exposure to relatively low levels of radiation, such as those experienced by millions of people after Chernobyl, causes little harm to the body. Some scientists even suggest that exposure to low-level radiation increases the body's ability to fight against other cancers.

> **"** Only three percent of those contaminated by Chernobyl will die from cancer, on top of the 25 percent who will die of cancer anyway. The overall health message is reassuring. **"**
>
> Michael Repacholi, radiation manager, World Health Organisation

## Finding sites

Whatever the truth of this, it is certainly the case that few people want to have a nuclear power station in their locality. Finding suitable sites for a new generation of nuclear power stations may prove to be a real hurdle for a revitalized nuclear industry. It would, in theory, make sense to build them on existing sites, since they already have what are known as *operating licenses*. However, not everyone would agree. Nuclear power plants are often built on coastal sites, close to sea level. Recent experiences of devastating tsunamis, together with predicted sea level rises due to global warming, may make these sites unsuitable in the future.

## Mental health

It may be surprising that some of the greatest damage caused by nuclear power (or at least, nuclear accidents)

has been to mental health. A report produced in 2005 by the United Nations suggested mental illness was the biggest public health problem caused by the Chernobyl accident. The families that were forcibly relocated to safer areas were deeply traumatized. Some suffered what was called *paralyzing fatalism*—an idea that life was no longer worth living. In some cases this led to reckless behavior, alcoholism, and even deliberately eating highly contaminated food.

### THE ARGUMENT:
### Nuclear power is safer than other energy sources

**For:**
- All technologies carry risk—nuclear power is no exception.
- It is probably true to say that more coal miners are killed in a year than have ever been killed in nuclear accidents.

**Against:**
- Nuclear power is unique in having the potential to cause death and illness on a huge scale in the event of a serious accident.
- It is hard to separate nuclear power and the development of nuclear weapons.

# CHAPTER 5 | The cost of nuclear power

Were the early supporters of nuclear power right when they said it would be "too cheap to meter"? While the cost of electricity generation through nuclear power appeared to be as good, or better than some of its rivals, it seemed that other costs were not always shown—particularly, the costs of "decommissioning."

## Decommissioning

It costs $2.8 to $4.6 billion to remove (or decommission) a nuclear power station—about twice the amount they cost to build. For obvious reasons, it is dangerous work.

> **"** [Delaying decommissioning] is leaving the problem for future generations, and throughout that period, you've got the problem of storage, safety, and security. **"**
>
> Sir Anthony Cleaver, U.K. Nuclear Decommissioning Authority

▽ 1956: Queen Elizabeth II opens the world's first commercial nuclear power station at Calderhall, Cumbria, England.

The removal is mainly carried out using remote-controlled equipment. Building materials from the plant, and spent fuel stored on site, have to be treated as high-level waste. The land is also likely to be contaminated. One solution would be to delay the job of decommissioning for 50 to 100 years until radiation levels are reduced.

## Cover up?

Even without decommissioning, other "hidden" costs have come to light. The extraction and fabrication of uranium fuel is expensive. Are these costs being accurately reflected in the figures that the public (and even governments) are being shown? Added to this is the issue of the disposal of waste—a problem still not resolved. It is estimated that the Yucca Mountain waste scheme alone could cost in the region of $48.7 billion.

Finally, it seemed that even some governments were implicated in the uncertainty over costs. In their eagerness to promote nuclear power, certain governments were accused of supporting the nuclear power industry through direct payments or subsidies, awarding long-term contracts and guarantees ahead of those who would pay the costs of waste disposal, and future decommissioning. The notion of cheap nuclear power is certainly over.

## CASE STUDY: Yankee Rowe

Decommissioning of the Yankee Rowe nuclear power station in Western Massachusetts started in 1993 and was completed in 2006. During that time, the majority of the existing buildings were demolished and removed to disposal or recycling facilities. Contaminated soil was removed or treated. Spent fuel was transferred from wet to dry "cask" storage in 2003. The 16 steel and concrete casks have to stay on-site until the U.S. Department of Energy removes the spent fuel to a "federal storage facility." Extensive risk assessments of the site have to be carried out to determine the danger of radioactive and nonradioactive contamination. The aim is to reduce danger to future users of the site to a cancer risk of an additional one case in 100,000. This, the site owners admit, may never be achieved.

△ Nuclear plants, such as this one in Dungeness, England, are about the same size and capacity as conventional power stations.

## Cost—fact or fiction?

So what is the real cost of generating nuclear power? Perhaps more importantly, how does this compare with other energy sources?

According to British Energy and British Nuclear Fuels (BNF), the cost of nuclear power generation, even including decommissioning and other costs, is 4 to 6 cents per kilowatt-hour. This compares with 6 to 8 cents for offshore wind production, and 3 to 5 cents for energy produced by onshore wind turbines. Coal and gas-fired plants are probably around 7 cents per kilowatt-hour.

This looks like a competitive price. Other groups, however, claim the cost of nuclear generation is at least three times the BNF figure, perhaps as much as 16 cents per kilowatt-hour.

How do these differences of opinion occur? They arise partly because there are many costs that are unknown or difficult to predict. For example, new generations of nuclear power stations will, inevitably, require new and better technologies—some of them as yet taxes, which are charges put on different forms of power generation that produce greenhouse emissions, also swing the economic balance back in favor of nuclear power.

> " A resurgence of interest in nuclear power, justified by voodoo [make-believe] economics, stands to... potentially derail renewable energy. "
>
> Andrew Simms, New Economics Foundation, U.K.

unproven and uncosted. There may be expensive delays in construction, for example, the Dungeness B power station in the south of England took over 23 years to complete (partly because of planning delays) and came in at 400 percent over budget.

## Changing costs

In fact, it is very hard to put an exact figure on how much the generation of nuclear power costs, especially in comparison with other energy sources. One reason is that energy prices change all the time. In 2003, an influential report produced by the Massachusetts Institute of Technology (MIT) concluded that the cost of electricity generated by nuclear power was about 60 percent higher than from traditional gas- and coal-driven power plants. But since then, the price of gas, oil, and coal has risen dramatically. In addition, carbon

## THE ARGUMENT: Nuclear power is no more expensive than many other forms of energy

### For:
- Modern cost comparisons between nuclear power and other energy sources now take into account decommissioning and other costs.
- Often it is other technologies (for example, fossil fuels and wind power) where true costs are hidden, while governments often subsidize the development of renewable energy sources.

### Against:
- The real cost of nuclear power, particularly the issue of long-term storage, is unlikely ever to be fully taken into account.
- Who would pay for the damage caused by a disastrous nuclear accident, or for policing a waste disposal site for 1,000 years?

## A different way of looking at cost

Even taking into account factors such as decommissioning and long-term storage of nuclear waste, cost is not the only issue to consider. We now know the world is facing an energy crisis, or rather, two energy crises. We are rapidly running out of reserves of oil and gas (but not coal), and at the same time, our dependence on using fossil fuels for energy is almost certainly causing serious disruption to the global climate.

▽ This island in the Maldives is protected against erosion due to rising sea levels by sea defenses. This may become common as global warming continues.

## The cost of global warming

If we continue to use fossil fuels at the present rate, increasing $CO_2$ levels are likely to mean a 37°F (3°C) rise in global temperatures by the end of the century—maybe more. The effects of this are likely to be catastrophic for our planet. We are already seeing dramatic changes in weather patterns and increases in the rate at which pack ice (where the ocean is frozen), and even the polar ice caps (particularly in Greenland), is melting. Melting of the ice caps will result in rising sea levels and increased flooding of low-lying areas, devastating many poor regions of the world, and requiring the construction of massive sea defenses.

Global warming may cause entire ocean currents to change or stop flowing altogether. An increase in storms, hurricanes, and other unpredictable weather events is also likely. Natural habitats will change and many animals and plants may become extinct or threatened.

It is impossible to put a price on these developments but, if environmental analysts could, they would need to be added to the cost of fossil fuels. Although the extraction and processing of nuclear fuel produces $CO_2$, looked at overall, nuclear power is a "low carbon" technology.

Most estimates suggest that, over what is known as a *full life-cycle*, emissions of $CO_2$ from nuclear power are about the same as those for hydroelectric (water) power. A 1,250-megawatt nuclear power facility would be likely to produce about 0.5 million tons (0.6 million tonnes) of $CO_2$ per year, compared with 11.8 million tons (12 million tonnes) for a comparable coal-fired plant. Even at three times the cost of oil or coal, nuclear power may yet seem cheap for the price.

## Power struggle

Nuclear power is firmly back on the political agenda. However, nuclear power generates only electricity. Therefore, it can supply only a

> " At the moment, all our cars, all our airplanes and most of our central heating systems depend on fossil fuels directly [i.e. not electricity]. Doubling nuclear power would reduce greenhouse gas emissions by no more than 8 percent. "
>
> Roger Higman, Friends of the Earth U.K., 2005

relatively small part of our energy needs. Scientists, even governments, are now talking about reductions in $CO_2$ emissions of 60 percent or more in order to combat global warming. Opponents of nuclear power consider its expansion not only costly and dangerous, but also irrelevant. Finally, like oil- or gas-fired power stations, nuclear power generates large amounts of electricity that needs to be distributed widely over a national grid. Many communities are now looking at ways of meeting their energy needs on a much more local scale, for example, through renewable sources, or what is known as *cogeneration* (combined heat and power). Eventually, nuclear power may find itself out of step with our modern needs.

# CHAPTER 6 — Looking ahead to a nuclear-powered future

Does nuclear power have a future? To answer this, we need to look at how nuclear technology is developing and where future demand and investment is likely to take place.

## Three generations

Nuclear technology has seen three main "generations" of nuclear power station: the gas-cooled design, Pressurized Water Reactors, and so-called advanced designs. These include Fast Breeder Reactors (FBRs), which use plutonium as fuel, and the Pebble Bed Modular Reactor, which uses hot helium gas passing over "pebbles" of uranium to drive a turbine directly.

Designs for the fourth generation of power station are still on the drawing board and will not be operational before 2020 at the earliest. These will probably have what are known as *closed fuel-cycles*, meaning much of the spent fuel can be used again.

## Fuel for the future?

At the present time, recycled or reprocessed uranium makes up 40 percent of world supplies. By 2015, however, this is likely to fall as stocks of old fuel run out and demand starts to outstrip supply. More uranium will have to be dug out of the ground, increasing the risk of environmental damage and radioactive contamination.

## CASE STUDY: Nuclear batteries

A small Alaskan town with a population of 700 could become the site for an experimental mininuclear power plant. The device, known as a *battery*, because it has no moving parts, would generate about 10 megawatts (10,000 kilowatts) of power—about 1 percent of a standard nuclear plant's output. The container would be sealed and run for up to 30 years without the need to replace the fuel. To do this, part of the reactor would have to act as a "fast breeder," converting U-238 into plutonium. Similar devices could be used in poor or remote areas in less developed countries, where electricity has to be generated using diesel generators.

An alternative would be to develop more FBRs, since these generate plutonium as they burn uranium, which can then be used as fuel. FBRs can extract up to 30 times more energy than other designs, but the technology is difficult and extremely costly. They are likely to become more attractive, however, as uranium becomes scarce. Countries such as India are now leading the way in new FBR technologies. Countries in the West are likely to follow.

▽ Although this modern water reactor is much safer than some of its predecessors, problems, such as waste disposal, still remain.

## Beyond fission?

Looking even further into the future, energy may one day be generated by joining atoms together (fusion), rather than splitting them (fission). This would copy the nuclear reactions going on in the Sun, where isotopes of hydrogen fuse into helium, with the release of energy. In theory, at least, the technology would be safer than conventional nuclear power (aside from helium, the main by-product would be neutrons). An experimental fusion machine is being built in France, but many believe the technology will never be economically viable.

### Shelf life

Most nuclear power stations have a planned life of about 40 years. In practice, many operate for longer than this. In the United States, more than 15 reactors have been granted licenses extending their operating lives from 40 to 60 years. In Japan, reactor lifetimes of up to 70 years are now predicted.

However, for economic and safety reasons, some nuclear power stations have been closed down early. This has occurred in the U.S., where reactor numbers have fallen from 110 to 103.

△ Wagons transporting spent fuel. The need to transport nuclear material may increase the likelihood of accidents or terrorist attacks.

In the U.K., the cracking of graphite blocks in the core of some gas-cooled reactors (for example, Hinkley Point nuclear power plant in Somerset, England) may also cause early closure.

Many nuclear reactors will come to the end of their useful working lives in the next 20 to 30 years. The question we now face is whether to build or not to build?

## A new beginning?

Between 1999 and 2004 only two new nuclear reactors were built worldwide. Uncertainty surrounding the safety and cost of nuclear power meant that many countries were hesitating before investing further in the technology required to develop a nuclear industry.

Now this is changing. In May 2006, there were 27 new reactors under construction. It is interesting to look at their locations. Most are situated in the less developed countries, such as China, India, Indonesia, and Vietnam. Few new reactors are being built in the more developed economies, such as Western Europe. It is also interesting to look at where new reactors are planned or proposed. Again, we find that the less economically developed countries of Asia and Eastern Europe dominate.

This is not surprising, since these are the areas of the world where the demand for energy is likely to increase the most. However, it is also true that these regions are some of the more politically unstable parts of the world, and this brings its own problems. Once again, concerns have been raised that, unless the proper safeguards are put into place, new nuclear power installations could potentially become the sites of terrorist attacks, accidents, or the development of nuclear weapons.

## The pendulum swings

Now it seems that the more developed nations of the world are poised to follow. In July 2006, the U.K. government announced an energy "review," indicating it was in favor of the "nuclear option." It announced that it was ready to relax planning laws in order to speed up the construction of new plants. Although the review made the same allowance for renewable technologies, such as wind power, many saw this as a green light for the expansion of the U.K.'s nuclear industry. In August 2005, the U.S. government awarded a range of nuclear power subsidies worth nearly $20 billion. However, in Europe, countries such as Germany, Sweden, Spain, and Switzerland still reject investment in new nuclear plants.

> **If the U.S. does not start investing in nuclear energy in the next decade, it will have neither the skilled workers nor the industrial infrastructure [buildings, equipment, etc.] for nuclear power to be a viable option.**
>
> Peter Lyons, Head of U.S. Nuclear Regulatory Commission

## Full circle

Today, the nuclear industry appears to be riding high again. The reasons are not hard to find. Oil and gas reserves are depleting (and becoming more expensive), and many countries are reluctant to depend on other parts of the world for their energy resources—what is known as *security of supply.* Nuclear power is less dependent on external sources of energy than conventional power stations. If a country can obtain, manufacture, or recycle its own nuclear fuel, it can become more self-sufficient in energy.

> " The government is going to have to stop looking for an easy fix to our climate change and energy crisis. There simply isn't one. "
>
> Jonathon Porritt, U.K. Sustainable Development Commission

▽ Global energy demand over the next 20 to 25 years is expected to increase dramatically, especially in parts of the world that are developing rapidly, such as Southeast Asia.

As we have seen, this is not the only factor pushing the balance back in favor of the generation of nuclear power. The threat of global warming looms over us all, and many scientists

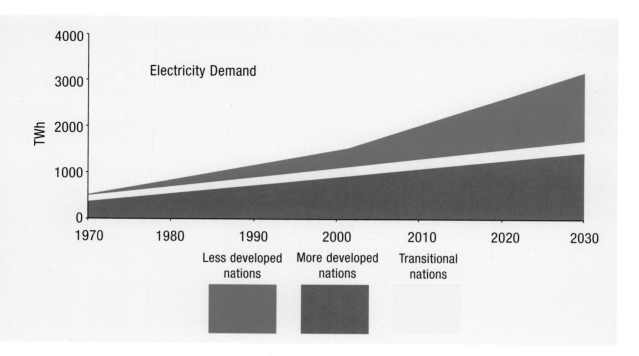

Electricity Demand

TWh

4000
3000
2000
1000
0

1970   1980   1990   2000   2010   2020   2030

Less developed nations    More developed nations    Transitional nations

## CASE STUDY:
## Finland—a test case?

The European Pressurized Reactor (EPR) in Finland is currently the only nuclear power station under construction in Europe. It is a relatively new design of pressurized water reactor, the kind that the U.K. might build if it continues to develop its nuclear option.

The EPR at Olkiluoto is being built jointly by French and German companies. It is owned by a Finnish company made up of industrial bodies that receive their electricity from the company itself.

There is a concern, therefore, that the new nuclear power plant will have a guaranteed market, and therefore will not have to compete in the Nordic electricity market. The project is due for completion in 2009 and many, including the United States, are watching with interest. By then it will become apparent whether the EPR design works well and how long it takes to build. In the United States and Europe, at least, a lot may depend on how well Finland's newest nuclear reactor really performs.

now believe that without significant reliance on nuclear power, the planet faces an uncertain climatic future.

What is clear is that we need to find alternatives to fossil fuels. The task has become an urgent and serious one. Nuclear power is not the only possible alternative, of course. Renewable energy sources could also supply some of the new energy mix. We could also significantly reduce our energy consumption by using more efficient technologies. As world energy demand rises, we have to face the prospect that neither, on its own, may be enough.

### The choice
Over the next five to ten years or so, individual countries will have to make their own decisions about their energy future. Many are likely to choose a mixture of conventional (fossil fuel), renewable, and nuclear sources.

This might seem like a reasonable option. Unfortunately, nuclear power tends to divide people into those who strongly support it and those who fervidly oppose it. A "middle way" may be hard to find. The important thing is to become involved in the debate and make up your own mind.

# Glossary

**Alpha radiation** Radiation that is harmful when inhaled, but unable to penetrate the skin.

**Atom** The smallest unit into which an element can be divided.

**Carbon tax** A charge put on fossil fuels to compensate for the effects of global warming.

**Cogeneration** Electricity generated by gas or oil, but the heat energy produced is used by local industry.

**Coolant** The liquid or gas into which the heat energy in a reactor is transferred, allowing it to drive turbines.

**Critical mass** The smallest amount of a nuclear fuel needed for nuclear fission to be self-sustaining.

**Decommissioning** When a power station reaches the end of its useful life and is dismantled.

**Energy gap** When the supply of energy sources worldwide, such as oil or gas, no longer meets global needs.

**Fossil fuels** Coal, oil, and gas formed over millions of years from the remains of plants and animals.

**Fuel fabrication plant** A facility where (nuclear) fuel is made.

**Gamma radiation** High-energy radiation that can be stopped only by thick lead or concrete cladding.

**Greenhouse effect** The warming of the Earth's climate due to gases in the atmosphere that trap solar heat before it can be radiated back into space.

**Heat exchanger** A device in which heat energy from one substance is transferred to another, without direct contact between the substances.

**Meltdown** When excess heat is produced during the process of nuclear fission, causing parts of the reactor to melt.

**National grid** The system of power lines that distributes a country's electricity.

**Nuclear fuel cycle** The process in which uranium is extracted, made into fuel pellets, and then reprocessed.

**Nuclear fusion** When atoms are combined at high temperatures, releasing energy.

**Reprocessing** Treating spent nuclear fuel and extracting the remaining uranium so that it can be reused.

**Sea defenses** Strong concrete barriers designed to withstand the sea.

**Subsidy** A payment, often made by a country's government, to support a particular technology.

**Turbine** A propeller-like mechanism turned by high-pressure steam and used to drive an electricity generator.

## Books

*Adventures in the Atomic Age* Glenn Seaborg; Farrer, Straus, and Giroux, New York, 2001: autobiography of the Swedish scientist who discovered plutonium.

*Fermi Remembered* James Cronin; University of Chicago Press, Chicago, 2004: account of the Italian scientist who first achieved sustained nuclear fission in 1942.

*Oppenheimer: Portrait of an Enigma* J Bernstein; Duckworth, London, 2004: account of Robert J. Oppenheimer who managed the Manhattan Project to develop the world's first atomic bomb.

*Nuclear Energy (Energy Essentials)* Steven Chpaman, Raintree Publishers, Oxford, 2005: a look at the place of nuclear power in today's society.

## Web Sites

Due to the changing nature of Internet links, The Rosen Publishing Group, Inc., has developed an online list of Web sites related to the subject of this book. This site is updated regularly. Please use this link to access the list:
www.rosenlinks.com/ted/nuclear/

# Index

Note: Page numbers in *italic* refer to illustrations.